Hodder Gibson

Scottish Examination Material

ENGLISH
Language Skills

for
Intermediate Level
Answers and Marking Schemes

Mary M Firth
Andrew G Ralston

Hodder Gibson

www.hoddereducation.co.uk

Orders: please contact Bookpoint Ltd, 130 Milton Park, Abingdon, Oxon OX14 4SB. Telephone: (44) 01235 827720, Fax: (44) 01235 400454. Lines are open from 9.00 – 6.00, Monday to Saturday, with a 24 hour message answering service. You can also order through our website www.hoddereducation.co.uk

British Library Cataloguing in Publication Data
A catalogue record for this title is available from The British Library

ISBN -10: 0 340 81206 0
ISBN -13: 978 0 340 81206 8

Published by Hodder Gibson, 2a Christie Street, Paisley PA1 1NB.
Tel: 0141 848 1609; Fax: 0141 889 6315; Email: hoddergibson@hodder.co.uk
First published 2003
Impression number   10 9 8 7 6 5 4
Year   2009 2008 2007 2006 2005

Papers used in this book are natural, renewable and recyclable products. They are made from wood grown in sustainable forests. The logging and manufacturing processes conform to the environmental regulations of the country of origin.

Typeset by Fakenham Phottosetting Ltd.
Printed by Hobbs the Printers, Hants for Hodder Gibson, 2a Christie Street, Paisley, PA1 1NB, Scotland, UK.

PART ONE: CLOSE READING SKILLS

UNDERSTANDING

Factual Questions

For Practice (pages 9–11)

1. *What **two** explanations does the writer suggest to account for the belief that some places are haunted?* (2 marks)

    a deliberate hoax
    a physical cause which is not yet understood
    (*1 mark for each*)

    Total: 2 marks

2. (a) *What are the **two** 'mysteries' which puzzle the writer concerning the building of John Harrison's first clock?* (2 marks)

    why Harrison decided to make a clock at all
    why he was so good at it although he had no training in clock-making
    (*1 mark for each*)

    Total: 2 marks

    (b) *What is unusual about the construction of the clock, and why did Harrison choose this form of construction?* (2 marks)

    it was made of wood and almost no other material
    Harrison was trained as a wood worker / he had wood available
    (*1 mark for each*)

    Total: 2 marks

3. *What **two** reasons does the writer give for smugglers pretending that their landing places were haunted?* (2 marks)

    it made people stay away from the place out of fear of the 'ghosts'
    it provided an explanation for any activity that was seen
    (*1 mark for each*)

    Total: 2 marks

4. *The writer states that his interest in football helped him fit in to his new school and get on with his schoolmates. What three facts does he mention that might have made things difficult for him?* (3 marks)

    he was the only boy who supported that particular team
    he was smaller than all the other boys in the class
    he looked childish as he wore shorts
    (*1 mark for each*)

    Total: 3 marks

5. *The author gives several reasons for his childhood being 'not altogether happy'.*

    (a) *Summarise the main ones.* (4 marks)

    he was an orphan, and might feel unloved
    he was an only child, so he would lack the company of siblings
    he lived with an elderly spinster aunt, so he would lack young companions

English Language Skills for Intermediate Level — Answers and Marking Schemes © Hodder Gibson.

his aunt lived in a rural area and did not do very much, which would have been dull for him

his aunt had few visitors, hardly ever went out and never went far afield, so he would have had little amusement

(Any four, 1 mark for each)

Total: 4 marks

(b) *Suggest* **one** *thing he mentions that might have cheered him up and explain why you think it might have done so.* (2 marks)

his aunt's house had a big garden (1 mark) where he could play and explore without being in any danger of causing damage as it was 'untidy' (1 mark)

his aunt had pets: 'two Persian cats' (1 mark) which might have been fun for a child to play with (1 mark)

(Any two, 1 mark for each)

Total: 2 marks

Tip

It is essential that answers to Understanding questions should be in the student's own words. Answers which are 'lifts', i.e. quoted directly from the text, should receive **no** marks, even if students have identified the correct part of the text.

Meanings of Words

For Practice (pages 13–15)

1. *traumatic*: emotionally wounding (1 mark); he lists a large number of upsetting personal problems such as his parents separating, moving house, being homeless, being ill and starting a new school (1 mark).

   Total: 2 marks

2. *finery*: personal adornment (1 mark); the writer lists examples such as silk dresses, flower trimmed hats and garlands of flowers (1 mark).

   Total: 2 marks

3. *subterranean*: underground (1 mark); the writer refers to mines, which are underground, and rumblings in 'underground darkness' (1 mark).

   Total: 2 marks

4. *conjecture*: guess / speculate (1 mark); reference to nothing being known and 'a secret that will never be revealed', hence any explanation must be a guess; the expression 'many people believe' shows they do not actually know, but are only guessing (1 mark).

   Total: 2 marks

5. *posthumous*: born after the father's death (1 mark); the euphemism for death ('father's eyes had closed') shows that his father died six months before he was born; reference to fact that father never saw him (1 mark).

   Total: 2 marks

English Language Skills for Intermediate Level — Answers and Marking Schemes © Hodder Gibson.

6.   *unpredictable*: erratic / could not be told in advance (1 mark); reference to how brother's behaviour varied from cheerfulness to depression, and that he sometimes threw the furniture (1 mark).

Total: 2 marks

7.   *congenial*: pleasant / welcome (1 mark); he enjoyed reading and writing; he felt safe from the bullies (1 mark).

Total: 2 marks

8.   *benevolent*: kind (1 mark); the lady saved Oliver's life; she was generous to him although she could hardly afford it; she spoke nicely to him (1 mark).

Total: 2 marks

ANALYSIS

Sentence Structure

For Practice (pages 17–18)

1.   Question

2.   Command

3.   Exclamation

4.   Question (rhetorical)

5.   Statement

6.   Minor sentence; exclamation / minor sentence

7.   Question

8.   Command

9.   Exclamation / minor sentence

10.   Statement

Tip

In a sentence structure question, it is never enough simply to identify a type of sentence such as a rhetorical question. The **effect** of the type of sentence chosen must always be explained.

Parts of Speech

For Practice (page 20)

Nouns: terror; finger
Adverbs: now; carelessly
Adjectives: ragged; pale
Verbs: touched; fell

English Language Skills for Intermediate Level — Answers and Marking Schemes © Hodder Gibson.

Prepositions: beneath; upon
Pronouns: he; it
Conjunctions: for; and
Articles: the; a

Sentence Structure / Punctuation

For Practice (pages 22–26)

1. *Show how the author uses sentence structure to emphasise the narrator's sense of shame and panic at losing his horse.* (2 marks)

    Following the two statements, the writer uses a series of exclamations which indicate his thoughts and emotions.
    The repetition of the opening words 'If only' in the first three exclamations is effective in adding further emphasis.
    The use of the exclamation marks gives an impression of very strong feelings.
    (*Any two, 1 mark for each*)

    Total: 2 marks

2. *How does Dickens use sentence structure to emphasise the dramatic way in which his character, Scrooge, has reformed?* (2 marks)

    He repeats phrases which include the word 'good' three times: 'as good a – '(1 mark).
    He builds up to a climax with the list of words: friend, master and finally 'man' which covers all aspects of Scrooge's character (1 mark).

    Total: 2 marks

3. *Show how the writer uses **two** features of sentence structure to emphasise the number of fairground rides the children went on, and how these get more and more daring.* (2 marks)

    Number
    She uses a list of short statements all beginning 'we went on', giving the impression of a large number of rides.
    The short statements are linked with semi-colons rather than full stops, which speeds up the list giving an impression of many things.
    (*Any one, 1 mark*)

    How they get more daring
    She begins a sentence 'We even . . . ' which suggests building up to a climax.
    The use of parenthesis ('plucking up our courage') shows how daring they felt the rocket launcher was.
    The use of italics '*turned upside down*' shows it was particularly frightening.
    (*Any one, 1 mark*)

    Total: 2 marks

4. *This comment is made about Bill Sykes's murder of Nancy in Dickens's 'Oliver Twist'. How does Dickens use sentence structure to emphasise the dramatic nature of the deed?* (2 marks)

    The two sentences begin with similar phrases 'Of all . . .' The repetition is dramatic.
    Both sentences use inversion, with the main clause coming last. This creates suspense and means the most dramatic information comes last and therefore stands out.

English Language Skills for Intermediate Level — Answers and Marking Schemes © Hodder Gibson.

Each sentence ends with a superlative: 'worst'; 'foulest'; 'most cruel' which provides a dramatic tone.
(*Any two, 1 mark for each*)

Total: 2 marks

5. *Show how the writer uses sentence structure to emphasise the huge extent of the crater of this giant volcano. (Look for sentence types, use of conjunctions and repetition. Use the punctuation as a clue).* (5 marks)

The exclamation mark after the first sentence alerts the reader to something special.
The second sentence is very long and complex with two parentheses, which imitates the width of the huge crater.
The first parenthesis is a list including both commas and the conjunction 'and' which seems to elongate it.
In the second parenthesis he uses repetition of 'on, and on, and on'. The use of a comma before each use of 'and' slows down the pace, making it seem even longer.
The addition of the phrase 'and far beyond' at the end of the long sentence suggests a huge distance.
The statements have the effect of exclamations because of the use of exclamation marks.
(*Mark on merit depending on detail of explanations*)

Total: 5 marks

Tip

As punctuation is what reveals sentence structure, the first thing to do when tackling a structure question is to identify the punctuation marks used in the sentence.

---

6. *Show how the writer uses sentence structure and punctuation to create a convincing picture of someone in a cinema plucking up the courage to complain to someone who is disturbing him by talking.* (5 marks)

He begins with 'Er' showing hesitation.
He repeats the expression 'Excuse me', suggesting he is persisting.
Each sentence following the phrase 'Excuse me' gets longer, building up to a climax, showing his exasperation coming out.
He starts using rhetorical questions in 'Do you mind?' etc. showing his anger and determination strengthening.
He breaks off with the incomplete 'Excus ... The ellipsis '...' shows him plucking up his courage to be more forthright.
The use of capitals in 'SHUT UP' followed by multiple exclamation marks and question marks expresses his anger bursting out.
(*Mark on merit depending on detail of explanations*)

Total: 5 marks

7. *How does the writer use sentence structure to emphasise the immense size of the sea monster?* (4 marks)

The sentence beginning 'and then' in line 5 is very long, and uses the technique of inversion, with the subject coming after the verb 'came'. The delay seems to spin out the length of the monster as the sentence is spun out.
The subject is a list of phrases separated with commas which slows the tempo and also creates a sense of length.

English Language Skills for Intermediate Level — Answers and Marking Schemes © Hodder Gibson.

The next sentence also begins 'and then': the repetition implies the monster is still emerging and so must be huge.

The parenthesis 'not a body' spins out the sentence. The repetition in 'more neck and more' emphasises the great length.

The exclamation mark emphasises the effect of the repetition.

The last sentence has the marker 'Only then' at the start to emphasise size.

The simile within the commas again spins out the sentence before the mention of the monster emerging fully.

(*Any four, 1 mark for each*)

Total: 4 marks

8. *Show how the writer uses sentence structure to show how time appears distorted to a small boy at boarding school who is desperate for the holidays to arrive.* (4 marks)

In the second sentence the writer begins with 'how', followed by a comma which makes a slow beginning. He spins out the list of 'months, weeks and days' by putting them in phrases separated by commas and linked with 'and' which slows the tempo.

The sentence then has a semi-colon. After the semi-colon the writer uses many separate clauses describing his fears which suggests time stretching out as if the holidays will never come. The conjunction 'and' is repeated alongside commas slowing the pace suggesting the idea of time as endless.

The last sentence is also very long with many phrases strung together showing his sense of time passing, but finally getting faster: 'tomorrow, today, tonight.' The tempo is increased by the use of commas alone, without 'ands'. The sentence ends with a rush after the dash as if his journey home seems to arrive suddenly.

(*Answer should note effect of sentence length, use of commas and conjunctions and listing effects of phrases and clauses*)

Total: 4 marks

9. *Show how the author uses sentence structure to create a sense of drama in this description of a volcano erupting.* (5 marks)

The length of the whole sentence imitates the action of the volcano, building up with lists of descriptive phrases like 'four or five feet high' and progressing to the final section after the dash, which is like the outflow of the volcano.

The use of inversion in 'up through them were bursting gorgeous sprays of lava gouts' creates drama by delaying the subject of the clause. Placing 'up' near the beginning of this clause emphasises the height of the eruption.

Repetition in the list of phrases 'some white, some red and some golden' suggests the repeated bursts of fire from the volcano, and gives an impression of large amounts of lava.

The phrase after the dash dramatically sums up the description of what has gone before.

The length of the last phrase with its many long words acts as a climax, ending with a dramatic expression with seven syllables: 'unapproachable splendour'.

(*Mark on merit for good detail with examples*)

Total: 5 marks

10. *Show how the author's sentence structure indicates the suddenness of the shooting and also presents the last moments of the victim realistically.* (4 marks)

The very short second sentence is extremely dramatic and emphasises the speed of the shot. Beginning the sentence with the same word as ended the first sentence creates a jerky, staccato effect which emphasises the suddenness of the shooting.

The structure of the last sentence imitates the fluttering breath of the dying man. It consists of a number of short statements, two of which are in parenthesis rather than being joined

English Language Skills for Intermediate Level — Answers and Marking Schemes © Hodder Gibson.

with 'ands' which gives a very jerky, awkward effect. The second parenthesis 'an extension' is a minor sentence, implying the fading away of his breath. The last two clauses then swiftly end the sentence as if with a dying gasp.
(*Mark on merit for detailed answer*)

Total: 4 marks

Expression and Word Choice

For Practice (page 29)

This article is full of informal, colloquial features. Find two or more examples of each of the following and fill them in to the table. One or two are filled in to help you.

'Command' type of sentence structure	1. Think of ... (line 1) 2. Meet Vincent van Gogh (line 4)
Sentences without verbs / lapses of written grammar rules	1. Philistine! (line 1) 2. Only the lobe. (line 4)
Informal expressions	1. that old chestnut (line 3) 2. hard-luck story (line 7) 3. a job 4. terrific (line 12)
Use of second person (you)	1. You think of ... (line 1) 2. You could talk ... (line 2)
Informal reference to a person (e.g., use of first name or nickname)	1. poor old Vincent 2. Vince (line 2) 3. Big Brother (line 19)
Abbreviations	1. let's begin (line 3) 2. didn't (line 3) 3. He's (line 5) 4. doesn't (line 5) 5. it's (line 15) 6. haven't (line 18)
Slang words or expressions	1. OK (line 4) 2. hits the pits (line 9) 3. bumming around (line 12)

English Language Skills for Intermediate Level — Answers and Marking Schemes © Hodder Gibson.

Dialect

For Practice (pages 30–31)

Compare the sections that are in Scots and English.
Write down in two columns the words that are completely different. The first pair are entered for you.

Scots	Standard English
gey	really
dreich	dismal
happed	wrapped
nap coat	top coat
pixie	bobble-hat
pawkies	mittens
bitter	cold
starve	freeze to death
wee	little
kidoan	pretend
skelp	slap

Shades of Meaning

For Practice (pages 33–35)

1. *Quote the word which suggests the writer is so embarrassed he does not wish to be seen.*
    (1 mark)

    slunk

    Total: 1 mark

2. *What does the word 'blundered' reveal about the way the speaker descended the stairs?*
    (2 marks)

    He moved clumsily / quickly / not placing his feet carefully / heavily.
    (*Mark on merit for clear explanation*)

    Total: 2 marks

3. *Explain the feelings the word 'feeble' arouses in the reader compared with a word like 'small'.*
    (2 marks)

    'Feeble' sounds as if the fire is lacking in warmth and strength as well as size (1 mark). It makes the whole image more pathetic and arouses sympathy (1 mark).

    Total: 2 marks

English Language Skills for Intermediate Level — Answers and Marking Schemes © Hodder Gibson.

4. *What does the choice of 'hoisted' reveal about the way the narrator moved his leg?*

(2 marks)

It suggests he found his leg heavy and awkward. His leg seems like an alien object rather than part of his own body.
(*Mark on merit for clear explanation*)

Total: 2 marks

5. (a) *What does the word 'sprawled' add to the picture of the way in which the man's body was lying?*

(1 mark)

It suggests the body is lying untidily, with the limbs spread out awkwardly, as if it had fallen.

Total: 1 mark

(b) *Explain how the word 'skewered' adds to the horror of the scene.*

(2 marks)

It has associations of meat, as a skewer is used like a spit for roasting meat. The body has been treated disrespectfully as if it is a piece of meat.
(*Mark on merit*)

Total: 2 marks

6. *What does 'cringed' tell us about the relationship between the two characters in this extract?*

(2 marks)

'cringed' means to shrink back in fear, so it suggests Tom is afraid of Mr Connor.

Total: 2 marks

7. (a) *What associations does the choice of 'shrouded' add to this scene?*

(1 mark)

Death. A shroud is a garment for a dead body. It adds a touch of horror.

Total: 1 mark

(b) *Compare the alternatives 'covered' or 'cloaked' instead.*

(2 marks)

'Covered' would be neutral, merely suggesting the body was not visible. (1 mark)
'Cloaked' is more dashing and glamorous with associations of highwaymen's cloaks etc. (1 mark)

Total: 2 marks

8. *How does the choice of 'gnawed' help you understand how the child ate?*

(2 marks)

'Gnaw' means to chew hard, usually on a bone. It suggests the child tore at the hamburger with its teeth as if it was starving.

Total: 2 marks

Tip

An answer to a word choice question should be precise. Comparing the word or phrase chosen by an author with a more neutral expression, as in examples 3 and 7(b) above, is a good way to show clear awareness of a precise shade of meaning. Students should be encouraged to do this even if the question does not specifically ask for it.

English Language Skills for Intermediate Level — Answers and Marking Schemes © Hodder Gibson.

Word choice to create atmosphere

Discuss (page 35)

Pick out all the words and phrases that imply this place is either unique or the best of its kind.

fabulous
best known
most famous
a greater wealth ... than can be found anywhere else
magnificent
with famous pasts
glorious

For Practice (pages 36–37)

1. (a) *What kind of atmosphere is created by the use of the words and expressions under-lined?*
(2 marks)

depressing / comfortless / sense of death or destruction / desolate etc.
(*Mark on merit for clear explanation*)
Total: 2 marks

(b) *Pick out any **three** expressions and explain precisely what each contributes to this effect.*
(3 marks)

Answers should be precise, e.g. 'leafless trees' suggests winter, with connotations of cold, misery etc.; 'sad' is an example of personification, suggesting the earth is unhappy at what the war has done to it.
(*Mark on merit for precision*)
Total: 3 marks

2. (a) *Explain how each of the two underlined phrases contributes to the sense that the new house will be a refuge to the family.*
(4 marks)

'an eiderdown of olive-groves' suggests the warmth and comfort of a quilt (1 mark) , as though the house will also keep the family warm and comfortable (1 mark).
'guarded by a group of tall, slim cypress-trees' is an example of personification, com-paring the trees to soldiers or watchmen (1 mark) which suggests the family will be kept safe in this house (1 mark).
Total: 4 marks

(b) *Pick out **two** other expressions which also add to the attractive nature of the descrip-tion by appealing to the senses. Explain which of the senses is being appealed to.*
(4 marks)

Answers should identify phrases and explain their appeal, e.g., strawberry-pink (1 mark); appeals to visual sense, as it implies a bright, cheerful colour (1 mark) / appeals to taste, as if the house is good enough to eat. (1 mark)
(*Mark on merit*)
Total: 4 marks

English Language Skills for Intermediate Level — Answers and Marking Schemes © Hodder Gibson.

3. (a) *Pick out any **two** phrases and show how they help create an uneasy, eerie feeling.*
                                                                          (4 marks)

    'a sodden morning' (1 mark): the weather is so wet that it is as if it will never be dry, which creates a sense of discomfort (1 mark).
    'a sickly light' (1 mark): the pale light is personified as if it feels ill at what is about to happen / makes people feel ill (1 mark).
    'the high walls' (1 mark): image is of being trapped which creates a tense claustrophobic feeling (1 mark).

    Total: 4 marks

    (b) *What hints do you think this opening description gives of the writer's feelings about the execution at this point?*   (2 marks)

    Answers should give supporting evidence e.g. 'sodden' suggests he feels uncomfortable and depressed at the prospect; 'sickly' suggests he feels ill at what is to come; 'high walls' suggests he himself feels trapped by his situation / he feels shut in and afraid because he cannot escape watching the execution.
    (*Mark on merit*)

    Total: 2 marks

4. *Describe the atmosphere of the schoolroom which the writer builds up. You should refer to at least 5 of the underlined expressions.*   (5 marks)

    Answers should analyse the effect of the phrases e.g. 'a long room' suggests an intimidatingly large place which makes the speaker feel small; 'strange unwholesome smell' makes the place sound unpleasant because of the sickly odour; 'mildewed', which means mouldy, gives the sense that the schoolroom is damp and neglected, and suggests the pupils will be neglected too.
    (*Mark on merit*)

    Total: 5 marks

5. *Underline or list all the expressions which you feel give a sense of tension building up.*
                                                                          (5 marks)

    'build-up of clouds'; 'a steady current of heated air'; 'rose all day'; 'thrust'; 'revolving masses of gas'; 'piled up the static'; 'ready to explode'; 'a brassy glare'; 'pushed in'; 'hot'; 'held no refreshment'; 'brooded'.
    (½ *mark for each reasonable example*)

    Total: 5 marks

For Practice (page 39)

Pick out all the words and expressions which you feel have an emotive effect. Then explain what emotions you feel they arouse in the reader.

Examples of emotive language:
Poverty can kill; cost you your life; shocking new statistics; monstrous unfairness; blights the future; dying at twice the rate; prosperous Milngavie; a deeply disturbing divide; the haves and the have-nots; your new-born baby; if you have the right postcode; the wean who enters the world; totally and utterly failed; expressed outrage; blatant inequality; callous indifference; the plight of the poor and underprivileged.

English Language Skills for Intermediate Level — Answers and Marking Schemes © Hodder Gibson.

Examples of appropriate explanations:
Headline 'Poverty can kill': personification suggests poverty is a murderer, an image which arouses fear and horror.
'Prosperous Milngavie': the writer hints that Milngavie enjoys a particularly privileged and comfortable existence, which arouses resentment and envy in the reader.
'If you have the right postcode': sneering tone arouses anger and resentment as it alleges snobbishness where certain areas are considered 'right' i.e. better.

For Practice (pages 40–41)

1. *Pick out all the words or expressions which are old-fashioned. Then try to think of how we would now express the same thing in Modern English.*

Old-fashioned	Modern alternative
a soft answer	a polite reply
turneth	turns / prevents
wrath	anger / offence
grievous	offensive / hurtful
the tongue of the wise	the voices of intelligent people
useth knowledge aright	express sensible ideas
the mouth of fools	the voices of silly people
poureth out foolishness	talk a lot of nonsense

2. • *What do you notice about the number of personal pronouns used?*

    There are no personal pronouns in the extract. Legal jargon prefers to use nouns to avoid any ambiguity.

    • *Usually we avoid repeating words to achieve good style. What is the case here?*

    Words and expressions such as 'payable' and 'units allocated' are repeated. No attempt is made to find synonyms to provide variety as would be the case in most other forms of English. The purpose of legal jargon is to communicate as precisely as possible.

    • *What do you notice about the length of the sentence and the number of punctuation marks used?*

    The sentence is very long and there are no punctuation marks other than the full stop at the end.

Figures of Speech

For Practice (pages 45–47)

1. *Show how the writer uses **comparisons**, **imagery** and **understatement** to suggest the tiny cabin in this old boat is claustrophobic and unsafe.*   (10 marks)

    Comparisons:
    'rather larger than a hearse' – although this is describing the size, the fact that the writer is comparing the cabin to a hearse, a vehicle for carrying the dead, makes the reader think of death, and therefore that the cabin itself may be a death trap.
    'One might swing a cat in it, perhaps, but not a long cat' – 'no room to swing a cat' is a proverbial expression for a confined space, showing the cabin is cramped. The humorous addition 'not a long cat' emphasises the lack of room.
    'It had two coffins on each side – I mean two bunks' – the writer pretends he has made a mistake, but the comparison of the bunks to coffins suggests not only their size and shape, but that sleeping in them would be dangerous and could lead to death.

English Language Skills for Intermediate Level — Answers and Marking Schemes © Hodder Gibson.

Imagery:
'as dark as a vault' – this simile makes us think of the dark of a crypt, a vault under a church which is used for storing coffins. This is a frightening image with overtones of death.
'Peopled the obscurity of a dungeon with ghostly shapes' – this metaphor compares the shadows cast by the lantern to ghosts which gives an eerie atmosphere, with more connotations of death.

Understatement:
'The floor room . . . was not extensive' – this is an understatement and implies the cabin was very tiny, and hence cramped.

Answers should reasonably explain references for 2 marks each.
(*Mark on merit*)

Total: 10 marks

2. *Pick out one example of **onomatopoeia** and one example of **assonance** in this extract and explain the effect of each.* (4 marks)

Onomatopoeia: bubbling; rushing; hissing; coughing; puffing

Assonance: churning rush

One mark for each example; one further mark for each explanation suggesting the sound imitates a particular noise of either the volcano or the paddle-steamer to which it is compared; e.g., hissing suggests the noise made by steam being forced from a narrow opening.

Total: 4 marks

3. *Show how the writer uses hyperbole to achieve a humorous effect in writing a critical review of this restaurant.* (4 marks)

'Three spoonfuls' exaggerates the tiny amount of soup but suggests the portion was ridiculously small.
'just visible at the bottom of a bowl': this is an extreme exaggeration to suggest you can hardly see the soup at all as there is so little.
'so small that one could probably have carved it off the fish while it was swimming along': this is impossible as the fish would be dead, but the extreme exaggeration creates a humorous effect.
'without it ever noticing': this is a humorous addition to the impossible idea that the portion of fish could be removed without troubling the fish at all.
(*Any two examples explained for 2 marks each*)

Total: 4 marks

4. *In this quotation from Shakespeare's 'The Tempest', two villains are planning to trick two other characters. Explain how this **simile** reveals the speaker is very confident they will succeed.* (2 marks)

The simile 'as a cat laps milk' is effective since cats by tradition are naturally fond of milk and will lap up a bowl of milk quickly. This suggests the people will accept the suggestions without even thinking about it.
(*2 marks for a clear explanation*)

Total: 2 marks

English Language Skills for Intermediate Level — Answers and Marking Schemes © Hodder Gibson.

5. *Pick out all the words which suggest **images** of a bird of prey and fire. How do these images help you to imagine the character of the old man?* (4 marks)

Bird of prey: hooded like a bird of prey; with a hawk's pride
Fire: blazing; flamed; a white. . .heat; burned
The images of the bird of prey suggest the man is cruel, vicious and arrogant, characteristics which a hawk is supposed to have; the images of fire suggest a damaging and destructive degree of ferocity and fanaticism.

Total: 4 marks

6. *What impression do you get of the couple from the first **simile** 'like two butterflies'? What difference does the change of simile after the dash make to this impression?* (3 marks)

'like two butterflies' suggests the couple are beautiful, but also fragile characters (1 mark) but changing this to 'a bee and a butterfly' has a comic effect and suggests one of the two was actually solid and capable, more practical than beautiful (2 marks).
(Mark on merit for a detailed explanation)

Total: 3 marks

7. *The writer is describing the tidal wave of muddy water following a dam bursting. To what extent is the **image** of the 'wall of lions' effective?* (3 marks)

The image of 'a wall of lions' is **effective** as it implies the dangerous, devouring nature of the floodwater. The adjectives 'shaggy' and 'tawny' belong to this simile and suggest the colour and texture of the water which is similar to lions' coats and manes in being yellowish brown and rough textured, as the water will be full of debris.

On the contrary, the image 'wall of lions' might be considered **ineffective** as lions do not form walls, and in fact the expression is almost like a mixed metaphor. The idea of lions forming a wall like bricks is slightly ridiculous as they are the wrong shape and the image is therefore unhelpful as it is not easy to picture.
(Mark on merit for a clear and detailed explanation)

Total: 3 marks

8. *Show how the writer has used **imagery** effectively to make the character of Dr No seem a terrifying opponent for James Bond.* (6 marks)

'as if they had been painted on as make-up for a conjurer': the artificial nature of Dr No's facial features makes him sound like a robot or alien creature who will be hard to overcome. 'conjurer' has overtones of magic and enchantment, as if James Bond may have to contend with supernatural powers.
'jet black eyes stared out of the skull': 'jet' is a hard black stone, and suggests that Dr No is made of harder material than flesh, and will not be vulnerable to harm. 'skull' meaning 'head' is a figure of speech (technically called 'synecdoche', which means a part is used for the whole) implying he is a death-like character, which inspires terror, like a ghost or the Grim Reaper.
'like the mouths of two small revolvers': this simile comparing his eyes to the barrels of guns implies Dr No is a deadly character. It also implies he is made of metal or something stronger than flesh.
'like a giant venomous worm': the idea of a huge worm is disgusting and unnatural. The idea of a 'venomous', or poisonous, worm makes him seem deadly as well.
(any three images clearly explained for two marks each)

Total: 6 marks

English Language Skills for Intermediate Level — Answers and Marking Schemes © Hodder Gibson.

Tip

In a question which asks the student to 'show' how techniques are used, as in examples 1, 3 and 8, it is essential that quotation be used to illustrate the points being made. Before writing the answer, students should be encouraged to list the required number of appropriate quotations in brief note form.

Structure of a Text

For Practice (pages 50–52)

Using the method explained on the previous page, show how each of the underlined sentences in the following extracts acts as a link. Each question is worth 2 marks. **(10 marks)**

1. The first part of the sentence 'it was such ecstasy to dream, and dream' refers back to the idea of sitting happily forgetting one's worries in the delightful atmosphere of the islands (1 mark); the second part 'till you got a bite' contrasts and moves on to the description of the swift action that was necessary following the scorpion bite (1 mark).

2. 'These children' refers back to the half-cast children mentioned earlier in the paragraph whose dead fathers had been soldiers (1 mark); 'an unenviable future' leads on to the explanation of why these children were to be pitied, namely that they were rejected by both Indians and Europeans (1 mark).

3. 'The dangers' refers back to the hazards of working in the mines mentioned earlier in the paragraph such as earth falls, flooding and poisonous gases (1 mark); 'were overcome' leads on to a list of the solutions such as better roof supports, water pumps and fires to improve the air (1 mark).

4. 'All this' refers back to the rapid changes in towns such as the building of factories and houses, the lack of cleanliness and the lack of concern for it (1 mark); 'became a very serious problem indeed' leads on to an account of the consequences such as disease and the deaths of thousands in epidemics (1 mark).

5. The second part of the link sentence 'the school buildings as they were to remain for the next century were complete' refers to the description of the main building of Madras College, the quadrangle described in the first part of the paragraph (1 mark). The phrase 'with one exception' links to the description of the building which was added as a girls' school and later used for Commerce and History which is described in the second part of the paragraph (1 mark).

Total: 10 marks

Tip

In a question on linkage, the answer should include **two** quotations, one linking back and the other linking forward. The answer should also briefly summarise the two points in the argument which these relate to.

English Language Skills for Intermediate Level — Answers and Marking Schemes © Hodder Gibson.

Tone

For Practice (pages 54–55)

1. Emotive

2. Ironic / tongue-in-cheek

3. Persuasive

4. Colloquial / chatty

5. Humorous

English Language Skills for Intermediate Level — Answers and Marking Schemes © Hodder Gibson.

PART TWO: PASSAGES FOR CLOSE READING

WATERY GRAVE ROBBERS

Questions (Page 60–64)

1. *Explain two ways in which the word 'dead' (line 3) stands out in the first paragraph.*

    (2 marks).

    Comment on the use of the dash (parenthesis)
    Use of contrast ('alive or dead')
    Climax: word 'dead' is the last in the sentence

    (Any two of the above for 1 mark each)

    Total: 2 marks

2. 'A watery highway of horror' (line 5)

    (a) *Explain **in your own words** what the writer means by this expression.* (2 marks)

    Canal provided a fast and direct route ('highway') for the transportation of the corpses.
    Total: 2 marks

    (b) *Suggest any **one** way in which the writer has made this phrase striking to the reader.*
    (1 mark)

    Either use of alliteration or use of word choice ('horror') to suggest a dramatic tone, as in a newspaper headline.
    The metaphor 'highway' emphasises the amount of traffic on the canal.
    The oxymoron 'watery highway' contains apparently contradictory ideas.

    Total: 1 mark

    TIP

    Questions that refer to the 'way' the writer makes a point will expect the student to make reference to the writer's technique.

    ---

3. *Give two reasons from lines 1–13 for large numbers of bodies being snatched from grave-yards at this period.*
    (2 marks)

    Medical schools in Glasgow and Edinburgh were expanding which created a greater demand for corpses for anatomy lessons; corpses could not be obtained legally; anatomists were prepared to pay good prices and did not ask questions about where the bodies had come from.
    (Any two for 1 mark each)

    Total: 2 marks

4. *Suggest a reason why the anatomy lecturers preferred to call the corpses 'subjects'.*
    (2 marks)

    It sounds more clinical / academic and therefore more legitimate; reference to technique of euphemism.

    Total: 2 marks

English Language Skills for Intermediate Level — Answers and Marking Schemes © Hodder Gibson.

5. (a) *Pick out any **two** words or expressions used in lines 14–15 to describe the boy who played the violin which particularly build up sympathy for him. Explain how each of the words or expressions arouses your sympathy for the boy.*   (2 marks)

poor: suggests he had to struggle to live
blind: he had not only to suffer an impoverished lifestyle but had the added hardship of a physical disability
orphan: fact he had no parents suggests that no-one cared for him
(*Any two for 1 mark each*)

Total: 2 marks

(b) *Explain **in your own words** why the grave robbers were particularly keen to obtain this particular boy's body.*   (2 marks)

Paraphrase of line 22: 'the boy's blindness made him an interesting "subject" for dissection.'
(*1 mark for basic point; second mark for some attempt at answering in own words*)

Total: 2 marks

(c) *Give **two** reasons why this boy's body would be difficult for the body-snatchers to obtain and one reason why it would be easy for them.*   (3 marks)

Difficult: (i) grave had been dug more deeply than usual; (ii) coffin was placed underneath another one   (2 marks)
Easy: only a low wall separated the graveyard from the canal, making it easy to load the coffin onto a boat   (1 mark)

Total: 3 marks

6. *'But all to no avail' (line 27)*
Show how this sentence acts as a link in the story of the blind boy.   (2 marks)

'All' refers back to the attempt to foil the robbers described in the previous paragraph (1 mark).
'To no avail' indicates that the precautions were unsuccessful; the rest of the paragraph makes clear that the grave was still robbed (1 mark).

Total: 2 marks

TIP

Questions asking for an explanation of how a linking phrase / sentence operates should refer to both what comes before the sentence and what comes after the sentence. A link must be joined at both ends or it is not a link!

---

7. *Burke and Hare moved on from stealing bodies that were already dead to murdering people in order to sell their bodies. What do the words 'dumped' (line 54) and 'carted' (line 55) suggest about their attitude to their victims?*   (2 marks)

'Dumped' usually refers to the disposal of unwanted material such as rubbish.
'Carted' usually refers to the movement of goods.
Both words suggest a callous, inhuman approach.

Total: 2 marks

English Language Skills for Intermediate Level — Answers and Marking Schemes © Hodder Gibson.

8. *'Up to £1,000 in today's money' (line 13); 'around £80,000 in today's money' (lines 46–47). Suggest a reason why the writer gives these payments for bodies in 'today's money'.*
(1 mark)

The reader can fully appreciate how lucrative the trade in bodies was at the time.
Total: 1 mark

9. *'Howling' in line 57 suggests the angry medical students made a noise like a pack of hounds. What other word in this paragraph continues this idea?* (1 mark)

'Bayed' (line 58).
Total: 1 mark

10. *Look at the role of Dr Robert Knox, the Professor of Anatomy in the story (lines 44–end). Referring closely to the text in your answer, show whether you feel the writer intends us to approve or disapprove of Dr Knox.* (2 marks)

Approval: Knox paid £200 for bodies but never received them; he is described as being 'no more unscrupulous than the other anatomists'.
Disapproval: when Knox received the body of Burke and Hare's first murder victim he asked no questions and complimented them on the freshness of the corpse; this praise was taken as an encouragement to go out and obtain more bodies by similar means.
(*Any two for 1 mark each. Answers may support approval OR disapproval OR a mix of both*)
Total: 2 marks

11. *Giving examples to support your answer, show how the writer has used any two of the following to emphasise the horror of the story of the trade in human bodies.* (6 marks)

word choice: many possibilities: 'grisly trade' (line 39); 'nasty secrets' (line 43); 'suffocated, stripped and dumped' (line 54), etc.
figures of speech: the metaphor 'a watery highway of horror' is effective as it emphasises the number of bodies which were being transported along the canal since a highway is a busy thoroughfare. The use of alliteration makes the expression stand out even more.
Irony is used in the first paragraph when he refers to 'passengers' and then says they may be 'alive or dead'. The dead 'passengers' are the corpses being illegally sent to the medical schools.
The writer also uses irony to describe Knox's response to Burke and Hare: 'he complimented them on the body's freshness.' This use of irony provides black humour since the body had in fact just been murdered by them.
use of examples: the blind orphan boy: reference to an individual that we know something about helps the reader to appreciate more fully the human suffering involved.
use of contrast and comparison: the expression 'alive or dead' in the first paragraph is an effective use of contrast. He begins the article with an apparently innocent account of the opening of a canal, and ends on a note of horror.
Expressions such as 'trade', 'supply' and 'fetched a good price' are typical of selling ordinary things in shops, and the contrast between the usual innocent use of such words and the fact that it is corpses which are being sold is macabre and effective. Similarly, the euphemism 'subjects' used by the anatomy lecturers contrasts with the word 'corpses' which expresses the horrific truth.
structure of the argument: the article begins by stressing the role of the Union Canal in the story of the grave robbers (lines 1–7); it then explains why there was a demand for corpses (lines 8–13); lines 14–34 deal with the case of the blind boy; lines 35 onwards show how the endless demand for corpses for dissection led to victims being murdered,

English Language Skills for Intermediate Level — Answers and Marking Schemes © Hodder Gibson.

focussing on the story of Burke and Hare; lines 60 onward explain how the trade came to an end.

Total: 6 marks

TIP

Answers to this kind of question should be marked flexibly: it is not necessary to find six individual points. There should, however, always be specific references and quotations: generalised points alone should score less than half the available marks.

TOTAL MARKS: 30

Focus on Structure (page 65)

1. *The passage opens with a reference to the opening of the Union Canal. What is the connection between this event and the rest of the story?* (2 marks)

    The connection is that the canal allowed the grave robbers to carry out their trade more efficiently.

    Total: 2 marks

2. *Read lines 1–13. Which one sentence best sums up what the first part of the story is about?* (1 mark)

    Lines 5–7: 'Bodies snatched . . . Glasgow.'

    Total: 1 mark

3. *Look at the second section of the story (lines 14–34). Explain clearly how this section relates to the opening one.* (2 marks)

    It provides a specific example of the general points explained in the opening paragraphs and shows the importance of the role played by the canal.

    Total: 2 marks

4. *Look at the seventh paragraph (lines 35–38). A new development in the story is described. What is this new development?* (1 mark)

    As robbing local graveyards did not meet the demands of the medical schools, corpses began to be imported from Ireland.

    Total: 1 mark

5. *Show how the sentence 'Yet . . . supplied' acts as a link at this stage.* (2 marks)

    'Yet' implies a contrast with the previous point. 'Such desperate stratagems' links back to risks taken by grave robbers; 'keep the medical schools supplied' links on to the details of the new sources of corpses which follow.

    Total: 2 marks

English Language Skills for Intermediate Level — Answers and Marking Schemes © Hodder Gibson.

6. *The last section describes the murderers, Burke and Hare. What phrase in the opening sentence of the eighth paragraph (lines 39–50) suggests that this will be the conclusion to the topic?* (1 mark)

'helped to end the grisly trade' (line 39)

Total: 1 mark

7. (a) *What new topic is introduced in the final paragraph to round off the article?* (1 mark)

How parliament took up the subject and passed new laws to deal with the problem.

Total: 1 mark

(b) *Explain how this provides an effective conclusion to the article.* (2 marks)

It is an effective conclusion as the legal availability of corpses for dissection meant that the incentive for criminals to provide bodies illegally no longer existed.

Total: 2 marks
TOTAL MARKS: 12

THE MIXED BLESSING OF ETERNAL LIFE

Questions (pages 68–69)

1. *In your own words, give two reasons why the old man was so lonely.* (2 marks)

he had outlived his friends; his family had moved away; he filled his time with activities which had no meaning for him
(*Any two for 1 mark each*)

Total: 2 marks

2. *Show how the author uses sentence structure to express her pride in being part of the modern generation.* (2 marks)

use of 'we' at the start of each sentence to place emphasis on the word; repetition of 'we'; use of the 'minor sentence' format (explained on page 17 of the book)
(*Any two for 1 mark each*)

Total: 2 marks

3. *In your own words, explain how the writer feels about the idea of the Ayrshire GP that young people should be given preference to older people in the allocation of medical treatment.* (2 marks)

'I find it hard to be shocked' – in other words, she agrees with his opinion
'I presumed it was an attitude that had always prevailed' – she feels that he was merely stating what everyone knew

Total: 2 marks

4. *'Marry quality with quantity.' What does this phrase suggest doctors should consider when deciding whether to keep a patient alive?* (2 marks)

The doctors have to balance up length of life with quality of life; how far is it worth prolonging the patient's life if the person will not be able to enjoy living longer?

Total: 2 marks

English Language Skills for Intermediate Level — Answers and Marking Schemes © Hodder Gibson.

5. *In lines 21–25, the writer compares the circumstances of two patients.*

    (a) *In your own words, explain **two** of the differences between these patients.* (2 marks)

One is young and has a child who needs looking after.
The other is elderly, frail and requires looking after him/herself.

Total: 2 marks

    (b) *The author does not state directly that she thinks the second patient should be left to die. Show with close reference to the text how she manages to suggest this without stating it directly.* (2 marks)

This is suggested (i) by listing all the problems the elderly patient is suffering, suggesting that the person has no quality of life and (ii) by the use of rhetorical questions.

Total: 2 marks

6. *Read lines 26–29. 'The older generation . . . theirs.'*

    (a) *Pick out two words or expressions (not whole sentences) which suggest that the older generation have common sense.* (2 marks)

'canny bunch'; 'clear-eyed understanding'

Total: 2 marks

    (b) *Quote the expression that shows the writer is not entirely sure that the elderly would choose not to be treated.* (1 mark)

'I dare say'

Total: 1 mark

7. *'Death is part of the package'. (line 31)*

    (a) *Explain what the writer means by this description of human life.* (2 marks)

Death is an inescapable part of life.

Total: 2 marks

    (b) *Explain how her choice of expression 'part of the package' affects her tone here.* (2 marks)

'Part of the package' introduces a more informal, colloquial or conversational tone.
Blunt or down-to-earth expression shows she is facing the facts.

Total: 2 marks

8. *'Our biblical span was three score years and ten'. (line 34) Give a reason why the author has used this form of expressing the number instead of simply saying '70 years'.* (1 mark)

Possibilities include:
A more stylish / literary way; this is the way that ages are expressed in the Bible, which she has just referred to; biblical reference implies that this is a fact that is long established / traditional.

Total: 1 mark

English Language Skills for Intermediate Level — Answers and Marking Schemes © Hodder Gibson.

9. *'The elderly get a big slice.'* Explain how the **image** the writer uses in this expression helps the reader understand how NHS resources are allocated. (2 marks)

The comparison here is between the allocation of resources and a helping of cake (1 mark). The size of the cake is limited; if one person gets a bigger slice, there is not so much left for others. In the same way, health service funding is limited and more money spent in one area leaves less to spend elsewhere (1 mark).

Total: 2 marks

10. *Look again at the first paragraph of the article (lines 1–5). Explain, with reference to the passage as a whole, how effective you find this as an introduction.* (2 marks)

The opening paragraph gave an individual case history which illustrates the general point developed in the rest of the passage: that spending money on prolonging the lives of very elderly patients may not be the best use of health service resources and may not necessarily bring any benefit to these patients.

Total: 2 marks

11. *With reference to any **two** of the following, show how well the writer has succeeded in putting across her argument that old people should not always be given medical treatment to prolong their lives: use of first person; word choice and imagery; sentence structure; use of examples; sense of personal involvement; emotive language.* (6 marks)

Many possibilities. The following is an example of an answer that would gain full marks. Note the use of specific examples to back up points.

Use of first person
The author uses the first person throughout the passage, often using the plural form 'we', as in 'those of us with any sense prepare to accept [our mortality] with all the grace we can muster'. This shows that the reader is aware that she is personally involved in the process and implies that she is facing the fact that one day she herself may be one of the elderly, frail patients she is talking about. This makes us more ready to go along with her argument.

Sentence Structure
Similarly, her use of sentence structure makes her approach more convincing: the frequent rhetorical questions lead the reader to feel that she has asked herself what her own answers might be. The use of expressions such as 'perhaps it is because' or 'But what if . . .' suggest that she has thought carefully about the various issues.

Total: 6 marks
TOTAL MARKS: 30

Focus on Persuasive Writing (page 70)

1. *Read lines 1–5. The writer begins with an anecdote.*

    (a) *Quote a phrase which might persuade the reader that the anecdote is true.* (1 mark)

    'The father of a friend once said'

    Total: 1 mark

English Language Skills for Intermediate Level — Answers and Marking Schemes © Hodder Gibson.

    (b)   *Pick two expressions which describe the old man which aim to arouse emotions such as pity in the reader.* (2 marks)

Any two of: lonely as a unicorn; his friends were dead; his family scattered; spent his endless days; he was itching for death.

Total: 2 marks

2.   *Why is the use of 'most of us' more effective at persuading the reader than 'most people' would be?* (2 marks)

This suggests that what she is saying does not only affect other people but affects her too. It also involves the reader.

Total: 2 marks

3.   *Read lines 15–20.*

    (a)   *Pick out two phrases the writer uses to describe those doctors whom she believes would stop treating the old.* (2 marks)

Great compassion; long experience.

Total: 2 marks

    (b)   *How does the use of these phrases help strengthen her argument?* (1 mark)

They suggest that these are doctors who could be trusted to make the right decision.

Total: 1 mark

4.   *Read lines 34–36.*

    (a)   *In this paragraph, the writer gives us a reason to be grateful for the length of life we now have. Explain the reason in your own words.* (1 mark)

Nowadays people tend to live on average ten years longer than in the past.

Total: 1 mark

    (b)   *Pick out the phrase which makes the reader want to belong to the group who are grateful.* (1 mark)

'Those of us with any sense'

Total: 1 mark

5.   *Read lines 38–39. What answer does the writer assume the reader will give to the question?* (1 mark)

She assumes the answer would be 'no-one'.

Total: 1 mark

6.   *'So let us be realistic.' Describe the writer's tone in this summing up.* (1 mark)

A reasonable, unemotional tone.

Total: 1 mark
TOTAL MARKS: 12

English Language Skills for Intermediate Level — Answers and Marking Schemes © Hodder Gibson.

EVEN BEGGARS HAVE CHIPS ON THEIR SHOULDERS

Questions (page 74–5)

1. *Look at the conversation between the writer and the 'grubby beggar'. (lines 2–13) Using quotation to support your answer, explain* **two** *differences between the styles of language used by the two speakers.* (4 marks)

   The beggar uses Scots dialect pronunciation, e.g. 'ur ye'. The narrator speaks with Standard English pronunciation, e.g. 'are you'.
   The beggar uses Scots words, e.g. 'aye' whereas the narrator uses Standard English words, e.g. 'no'.
   The beggar uses slang, e.g. 'brill', whereas the narrator speaks in Standard English without using slang, e.g. 'can't afford it'.
   The beggar uses a familiar, slightly cheeky tone, calling the narrator 'Big Man'; saying 'shame ye're no comin', whereas the narrator is more formal and distant, e.g. 'Thank you.'
   The narrator's language is hesitant and unsure shown by 'Um' and the use of ellipses '. . .', whereas the beggar is more confident, shown by the exclamation mark in 'Aye!'.
   (*Any* **two** *for 2 marks each; 1 mark for explaining difference, 1 for examples*)

   Total: 4 marks

2. *Explain why the beggar's words 'shame ye're no comin' seemed ironic to the writer.*
   (2 marks)

   He has just given money to the beggar who has tickets for an expensive concert which he himself hasn't been able to afford.
   (*2 marks for clear explanation*)

   Total: 2 marks

3. *Read lines 14–15 'The Big Man . . . cursing'.*
   In the next sentence the writer admits this part of the story is untrue. Give **one** *reason for him choosing to end the story of the encounter in this way, although it is untrue.* (2 marks)

   It reveals how angry he felt at having given money to the beggar who was obviously not that badly off.
   It humorously presents his thoughts of what he would like to have done, but didn't have the courage to do.
   It provides a funny false trail in the story before he admits he didn't really do it.
   (*One reason explained for 2 marks*)

   Total: 2 marks

4. *Read lines 17–21. 'The thing is . . . kilos of blankets'.*
   In your own words, explain why the writer feels he was wrong to be angry with the beggar.
   (2 marks)

   He realises that having handed over the money it is now up to the beggar to decide what he needs (1 mark). Beggars need other things than the obvious ones of tea and blankets (1 mark).

   Total: 2 marks

English Language Skills for Intermediate Level — Answers and Marking Schemes © Hodder Gibson.

5. *Read lines 39–45. 'Of course ... have been understandable.'*
    Can you suggest a serious point the writer may be making about the beggars who refused
    the offer of free pizza? (2 marks)

    Since the beggars seem so choosy about the type of free food offered, they are probably
    not really all that hungry.
    (*2 marks for clear explanation*)

    Total: 2 marks

6. *Show how the context helps you understand the meaning of 'take umbrage' in line 49.*
    (2 marks)

    'Take umbrage' means to take offence (1 mark). The beggars chased him after he had
    argued with them over using his mobile phone, showing he had offended them (1 mark).

    Total: 2 marks

7. *Read lines 51–54 'The incident ... in vogue'.*
    Pick out **two** *expressions from these lines which might have suggested people would be in*
    a peaceful, happy mood, and explain why each of them has this effect. (2 marks)

    'A summer evening' sounds warm and pleasant, a time when people would usually be feel-
    ing cheerful (1 mark). 'Edinburgh's meadows' sounds tranquil, like a country scene
    (1 mark).
    (*references to 'on the grass' or 'little dogs' worth half a mark each*)

    Total: 2 marks

8. *The writer could have used 'got' instead of 'lurched' in line 62. Explain what 'lurched' adds to*
    the picture of the beggars. (2 marks)

    'Lurched' suggests they got up unsteadily and drunkenly. This makes the beggars sound
    more formidable.
    (*2 marks for clear explanation*)

    Total: 2 marks

9. *'Spraying beer and curses'. (line 63)*
    Explain how the word 'spraying' is used both literally and figuratively in this phrase.
    (4 marks)

    'Spraying' is used literally of the beer, which the beggars would be spitting out of their
    mouths when they started shouting at the narrator (2 marks).
    'Spraying' is used figuratively of the curses, to mean that the beggars were shouting out a
    lot of swear words at the same time as they were spitting out the beer (2 marks).

    Total: 4 marks

English Language Skills for Intermediate Level — Answers and Marking Schemes © Hodder Gibson.

10. *Show how the writer uses sentence structure in the last paragraph to achieve a humorous effect.* (2 marks)

The first sentence is long, emphasised by the number of clauses and phrases which are linked by 'and'. This humorously suggests his long run to escape the beggars.
The parenthesis in brackets 'or an early grave' adds a witty aside.
The taunt in the direct speech is comical especially when he adds the word 'wittily' as if he is admiring his own coolness for shouting back although he was outnumbered by the beggars.
The minor sentence 'From a mile away' is funny as it reveals he wasn't so brave after all since he only dared to make the remark when he felt he was in no danger of being caught.
(*Any two points for 1 mark each*)

Total: 2 marks

11. *Looking at the passage as a whole, show how the author reveals his attitude to beggars. Discuss his use of **two** of the following: direct speech; exaggeration (hyperbole); use of examples; word choice; irony; humour.* (6 marks)

Sample answers:
Direct Speech: He is a little afraid of beggars. When he speaks to the 'grubby beggar' he sounds nervous. He says 'thank you' although he has given the beggar the money and seems quite hesitant in talking to him: 'Um'. He seems nervous when he offers the pizza: ' "Here you go," I ventured.'
Hyperbole: He dislikes beggars for pretending to be worse off than they are: 'as if I was handing him a live rattlesnake'. He does feel some sympathy, with his references to 'spending their entire lives running to the toilet' and 'trapped under several kilos of blankets' suggesting we don't always understand what beggars really need.
(*For 3 marks, a statement about his attitude and at least two examples should be given. Mark on merit: marks could be allocated 4 and 2*)

Total: 6 marks

Tips

An evaluation question like number 11 must be supported by quotation.
Using sub-headings is also helpful to the marker. In a question like number 11 which asks students to select two topics for discussion, they should be advised to write down and underline the topics chosen.

TOTAL MARKS: 28

English Language Skills for Intermediate Level — Answers and Marking Schemes © Hodder Gibson.

Focus on Humour (page 76)

1. *Look at the description of the writer's encounter with the beggar (lines 1–16).*

   (a) *Show how the writer presents a contrast between himself and the beggar, in which the beggar appears more secure and confident.* (4 marks)

   The beggar initiates the conversation, asking him for money.
   The beggar adopts a familiar, rather cheeky tone, calling him 'Big Man'.
   The narrator speaks in a 'mumbling, embarrassed fashion' showing he is ill at ease.
   The beggar continues to make conversation, asking him if he is going to the concert, taking the initiative and therefore seeming more confident.
   The narrator stumbles as he speaks 'No. Um . . .'
   The beggar adopts a patronising tone with the narrator: 'Shame ye're no comin.`
   (*Any four or similar, for 1 mark each*)

   Total: 4 marks

   (b) *Considering their positions in society, why is this contrast comical?* (1 mark)

   The narrator being better off and employed might be expected to have more self esteem than the beggar. Begging is generally considered to be humiliating.

   Total: 1 mark

   (c) *Briefly mention another example from the passage where the writer makes himself ridiculous by coming off worst in an encounter.* (1 mark)

   He offers the pizza to the homeless man and his offer is loudly rejected; the two younger beggars accept the pizza, but do so rudely and ungratefully; the group of drunken New Age-style beggars chase him since he was using a mobile phone.
   (*Any one for 1 mark*)

   Total: 1 mark

2. *Read lines 17–21. 'The thing is . . . kilos of blankets.'*
   Pick an example of hyperbole from these lines and describe its effect. (2 marks)

   'The poor fellas would spend their entire lives running to the toilet.' This is a ridiculous and comic image of beggars who can do nothing else since they have drunk so much tea. 'Trapped under several hundred kilos of blankets': this is comic as it is impossible, since the beggars would suffocate if they were under such a mountain of blankets.
   (*Any one explained for 2 marks*)

   Total: 2 marks

3. *A pun is a play on two meanings of the same word. Explain the pun on the word 'chips' in line 46.* (2 marks)

   'chips on the shoulder' mean grudges (1 mark); 'chips' are also chipped potatoes (1 mark).

   Total: 2 marks

4. *A common feature of humorous writing is where a writer presents a ridiculous episode as if it is true. Pick out an example of this from the passage and explain how much truth you feel there is in the story, and how much of it is invention.* (2 marks)

   Various possibilities, such as: the incident with the New Age-style beggars: the situation of the beggars shouting abuse at him for having a mobile phone seems realistic. However, it

English Language Skills for Intermediate Level — Answers and Marking Schemes © Hodder Gibson.

is likely that he made up the story of his comment to them and the chase. His speaking to them from 'a mile away' is impossible and so must be an exaggeration.
(*Mark on merit*)

Total: 2 marks
TOTAL MARKS: 12

ENGLISH SPOKEN HERE – AND THERE AND EVERYWHERE

Questions (pages 80–81)

1. *Read lines 1–14. 'So, what have the English . . . itself.'*

    (a) *'So, what have the English ever done for us?' (line 1)*
        Make clear what the tone of these words suggests about the attitude of the writer towards the English.   (2 marks)

        The tone is sarcastic / ironic (1 mark). It suggests the writer feels the English have not done much for us (1 mark).

        Total: 1 mark

    (b) *From lines 1–10, explain in your own words one advantage the Scots have gained from being linked with England.*   (2 marks)

        Some Scots have become rich (1 mark) from helping with the administration of the British Empire with its world-wide opportunities (1 mark).
        More money is spent per head on the health of Scottish people than on English people (1 mark) from money raised in taxes from the country as a whole (1 mark).
        The Scots have more say in Parliament (1 mark) as there are more Scots MPs per head of their population than English ones (1 mark).
        Scots benefit from the strength of the armed forces (1 mark) which are paid for with the resources of the United Kingdom as a whole (1 mark).
        Individual Scots who are cabinet ministers for the country as a whole have much more power than they would have if they had the same jobs in Scotland alone (2 marks).
        (*Any one for 2 marks*)

        Total: 2 marks

    (c) *The style of the first three paragraphs is based on a piece of dialogue from the film 'Life of Brian'. Quote **two** expressions which seem to you typical of **spoken** English.*   (2 marks)

        'So'; 'Well'; 'all that stuff'; 'Okay; yes'; 'then there's the bit about'; 'there's' (as an abbreviation); 'Oh yes'; 'Plus obviously'; 'Yes, yes, yes!'
        (*Any two for 2 marks. Quoting of rhetorical questions or minor sentences should also gain credit.*)

        Total: 2 marks

2. (a) *The word 'supple' (line 15) is usually applied to the body, and means strong and flexible. Explain what you think the author means by a language being 'supple'.*   (1 mark)

        It can be manipulated into many different forms such as dialects (1 mark).

        Total: 1 mark

English Language Skills for Intermediate Level — Answers and Marking Schemes © Hodder Gibson.

(b) *In lines 16–17, the author lists four English language writers, each of whom comes from a different country within the United Kingdom. Explain how this helps reinforce his point about English being a 'supple' language.* (2 marks)

The four writers all come from different corners of the country and write in very different styles (1 mark), yet they are all recognisably using the same basic forms and grammar of 'English' (1 mark).

Total: 2 marks

3. *In lines 17–18 the author claims English is 'the mother tongue of the world.' Referring to any one of the incidents described in lines 19–27, show how the anecdote helps prove this statement true.* (2 marks)

Since the Norwegian woman did not realise the diving instructor was also Scandinavian, she tried English first rather than her own language as she knew it would be much more widely understood. The man did understand English.
When German tourists wanted to communicate with a Greek waiter they used English as that was the only language they all understood.
When the Englishman in Oman was trying to communicate with a waiter in Arabic, and it turned out that the waiter was a Pakistani, English was the one common language in which they could communicate.
(*Any one example for 2 marks*)

Total: 2 marks

4. *Read lines 28–35. 'The International Herald Tribune ... occupation.'*

(a) *What is revealed about the attitude of the French and Germans to the dominance of the English language in Europe?* (1 mark)

They resent it / get angry about it, as it says 'to the irritation of ...'

Total: 1 mark

(b) *The number of signs in English on the streets of Paris is compared to the number of signs seen there in German during the Nazi occupation. Explain how this comparison helps emphasise the large number of English signs.* (1 mark)

When the Germans were in control, they would try to change all the signs to German, so this implies there are so many signs it is as if the English have conquered Paris.

Total: 1 mark

5. *Explain how the context helps you to arrive at the meaning of 'mandatory' (line 39).* (2 marks)

Mandatory means required / obligatory (1 mark). The word is contrasted with the phrase 'are an asset' which means an advantage, but not essential (1 mark).

Total: 2 marks

6. *Read lines 40–44. 'A few years ago ... money.'*
In your own words, explain the advantages a Chinese person would hope to gain from being fluent in English. (2 marks)

They would hope to get a job outside China (1 mark). This would give them the chance to earn very high salaries (1 mark).

Total: 2 marks

English Language Skills for Intermediate Level — Answers and Marking Schemes © Hodder Gibson.

7. *Look at the opening sentence of the tenth paragraph 'There is even . . . English (lines 45–47).*
Which word in this sentence emphasises how strange it is that Chinese people gather in a park to practise speaking English? (1 mark)

Even

Total: 1 mark

8. *Look at the next two sentences 'Can you imagine ... to improve their French?' (lines 47–49)*
*Identify and explain **two** further techniques the author uses in this section to demonstrate the strangeness of the Chinese practising English in the park.* (2 marks)

Rhetorical question creates incredulity: 'Can you imagine ...' (1 mark).
He gives examples of British public places such as Glasgow Green where the idea of people meeting to practise a foreign language would be absurd (1 mark).

Total: 2 marks

9. *Show how the sentence 'But maybe . . . lost control of it to America' (lines 57–58) acts as a link in the argument at this point.* (2 marks)

The expression 'Britain has given its language to the world' links back to his previous points about English being an international language (1 mark). The expression 'lost control of it to America' leads on to his next point which is the Americanisation of English (1 mark).

Total: 2 marks

10. *Show how the author uses sentence structure in the last paragraph (lines 61 – 62) to create a satisfactory conclusion.* (2 marks)

He begins by asking a question: 'So what ...' He then appears to answer with the words 'the world's dominant language.' This seems to imply English and he confirms this with a one word sentence 'English'. However he adds a twist by adding a further minor sentence with a modification: 'American English'. This is humorous as it seems to undercut his argument about English being the top language.
(2 marks for at least two points)

Total: 2 marks

11. *Looking at the article as a whole, show how the author has presented the topic effectively by his use of two of the following: colloquial English; tone; examples; personal involvement; a 'twist' at the end.* (6 marks)

A suitable answer worth full marks might be:

Personal Involvement: The anecdotes describing how English is used as an international language by people of different nationalities are made convincing by the fact that these are presented as personal experiences, marked by phrases such as 'recently I heard ...' The fact that he was working in China 'filming a documentary' explains why one Chinese man started speaking to him about listening to the BBC, and another approached him looking for a job. The fact that Esler has been in China several times lends authority to his views and observations on how English is widely used and respected abroad.

A twist at the end: The word 'But' at the beginning of the second last paragraph suggests a contradictory point is about to be made. He suggests Britain is no longer in control as American expressions are taking over. He lists examples firstly of expressions and then of

English Language Skills for Intermediate Level — Answers and Marking Schemes © Hodder Gibson.

pronunciations to support his argument. The passage ends humorously when he appears to be making the same point as at the beginning by saying 'England has given us the English language'. However, the last minor sentence 'American English' shows he does not believe that, and that he knows America is taking over our language. The whole argument is therefore turned on its head.
(*Mark flexibly on merit either as 3 and 3 or 4 and 2*)

Total: 6 marks
TOTAL MARKS: 29

Focus on Tone (page 82)

1. *The writer opens the article with a question to which he immediately gives an answer: 'Well nothing, obviously.'*

    (a) *Which word best describes the tone of this answer: ironic; sad; humorous; severe?*
                                                                           (1 mark)

    ironic
    Total: 1 mark

    (b) *Explain how the sentence immediately following the answer reinforces this tone. Comment on at least one of the following expressions: 'except'; 'vast amounts of money'; 'the most successful empire in history'; 'from Barbados to Ottawa to Hong Kong.'* (2 marks)

    The tone is reinforced by detailing huge advantages which are obviously not 'nothing' (1 mark). After 'except' you expect some minor advantage, not large ones; other references are examples of prosperity and wide opportunities in a large world-wide empire (1 mark).
    Total: 2 marks

2. *The same pattern of question / answer / development is used in paragraph two.*

    (a) *What does the tone of expressions like 'all that stuff' and 'the bit about' suggest about the writer's opinion of the English?* (1 mark)

    He appears to be dismissing their contributions as of little value.
    Total: 1 mark

    (b) *What do you think is the writer's actual opinion of the ways in which Scotland has been affected?* (1 mark)

    He believes Scotland has gained many advantages such as wealth and opportunities for personal advancement from the association with England.
    Total: 1 mark

3. *In lines 2–3 and 9 the writer uses superlatives: 'most successful'; 'strongest'.*

    (a) *Pick out **two** more examples of this from lines 11–14 and from lines 15–18.*
                                                                           (2 marks)

    greatest; most extraordinary; most supple.
    Total: 2 marks

English Language Skills for Intermediate Level — Answers and Marking Schemes © Hodder Gibson.

(b) Which **two** of the following words best describe the tone created by such superlatives: *objective; neutral; positive; ironic; grudging; admiring.*   (2 marks)

positive; admiring.

Total: 2 marks

4. *Throughout the article the writer has described the benefits of the English language to the world. Describe the tone of the last phrase 'American English' and explain how it affects the rest of the article.*   (3 marks)

Tone: 1 mark for appropriate tone such as humorous; tongue in cheek; witty.
It affects the rest of the article as he had previously seemed to see the English and their language as leading the world. The final admission that their language has been taken over by the Americans suggests he realises Britain is now insignificant compared with America, and that America is really the dominant culture.
(*2 marks for a clear explanation*)

Total: 3 marks
TOTAL MARKS: 12

English Language Skills for Intermediate Level — Answers and Marking Schemes © Hodder Gibson.

PART THREE: TEXTUAL ANALYSIS

For discussion (1) page 85

Similarities between two extracts:
- Both describe how actively the baby is moving about in the womb

How do they differ?
- The first conveys a sense of movement through description and comparison; the second takes a factual, scientific approach, showing how the movements develop over a period of time

What effects does the poet achieve which are not attempted in the prose passage?
- Poet uses numerous comparisons to help the reader visualise the movements and to imagine the feelings of the baby
- Poet is personally involved: 'my little loaf'
- Poet shows her affection through humour: 'a sprat in a pickle jar'
- Poet uses interesting sound effects: 'creel of eels'

For discussion (2) page 86

Shelley: uses personification to suggest the wind is a living force
simile of 'like ghosts' gives the description a supernatural dimension

Coleridge: use of repetition to convey how the ship is trapped in the ice
use of personification to convey the idea that the ice is like a dangerous and threatening animal
use of onomatopoeia to represent noises made by ice

Hardy: repetition of 'every' stresses how thoroughly everything is covered by the snow
'mute' implies personification

Browning: conversational tone: 'Well now'
simile of bull's horn developed in line 2 with the comparison of the mountain's edge to the creature's skull: suggests how visible the villa was

English Language Skills for Intermediate Level — Answers and Marking Schemes © Hodder Gibson.

WHAT IS POETRY?

1. Economical Use of Language

Example (page 88)

There are up to eleven different images. The four examples given here show the kind of comments that might be made.

EXAMPLE	FIGURE OF SPEECH	WHAT THE BABY IS COMPARED TO	WHAT THIS TELLS US ABOUT THE BABY
Clownlike	Simile	Baby is compared to a clown	Similar movements: clown turns somersaults, etc. Clown also has connotations of entertainment, laughter, etc. and the comparison implies the baby is happy
Wrapped up in yourself like a spool	Simile	The baby curled inside the womb is compared to thread or film wound round a reel	Comparison implies how tightly the baby is fitted into the womb
My little loaf	Metaphor	Baby is compared to a loaf of bread	The yeast in the bread causes it to expand and rise; similarly, the baby is growing within the womb
Snug as a bud	Simile	Baby is compared to the bud of a flower	Just as the petals of the bud are tightly packed and then open out in full flower, so too the baby is packed inside the womb and then emerges in birth

English Language Skills for Intermediate Level — Answers and Marking Schemes © Hodder Gibson.

2. Expression of Feelings

(page 89)

Make a list of the feelings and emotions you notice here, then write down the words and phrases used to convey these feelings.

Possibilities include:

Satisfaction	Jack fell as he'd have wished
	Her weak eyes/Had shone with gentle triumph
Appreciation	The Colonel writes so nicely
Bottled-up emotion	The tired voice that quavered to a choke
Pride	We mothers are so proud
Respect/tact	Quietly, the brother officer went out
Hypocrisy	He'd told the poor old dear some gallant lies
Contempt	Jack, cold-footed, useless swine
Guilt/shame	And no-one seemed to care

3. Element of Pattern

(page 90)

What do you notice about the pattern and structure of these extracts from three well-known poems?

Coleridge:	repetition to stress the utter loneliness
Tennyson:	repetition stresses how trapped the lady felt: the castle was a prison to her
Lawrence:	alliteration on 's' sound imitates the sound of the snake
	from the structural point of view, the long winding sentence structure reflects the shape of the snake

English Language Skills for Intermediate Level — Answers and Marking Schemes © Hodder Gibson.

PART FOUR: PRACTICE IN TEXTUAL ANALYSIS

The Competition

(page 92–95)

- *Write down details from the poem which help to locate the incident in a real place and at a particular time.*

    Hamilton; Leyland bus; Eddlewood; Cousar's Coup; Hurricane; tenements; Shotts Miner's Welfare Harriers Club; etc.

- *What are Douglas Dunn's feelings towards each of the following people?*

Character	Feeling	Evidence
Boy on the bus	feels they have something in common	'I couldn't help it; I had to talk to him'
The city cousin	contempt as the poet and his friends play a trick on him	Lines 6–8
Boy's mother	he presumably resents her protecting the boy	'His mother pulled him towards her'
Dunn's grandfather	affection / respect	'My grandfather wouldn't give him sixpence'
The athlete	determined to prove he is as good as his rival, whom he takes to be the boy he met on the bus years before	'I'd trained my spikes to ruin, convinced / My best competitor was him'

- *What point do you think Douglas Dunn is making [at the end of the poem]?*

    If the athlete had turned out to be the boy, there would have been a neat sense of justice to the story. Dunn may be saying here that life is rarely as simple and clear-cut as that: people are to be treated as individuals rather than as representatives of a particular social group.

- *What figures of speech are used in the examples? What kind of picture do these lines bring into your mind?*

    'Zoomed at his war games in the seat at front': onomatopoeia of 'zoomed' creates a picture of the boy flying the model aircraft and making accompanying engine sounds.
    'As brown as the manure in Cousar's coup': the simile compares the colour of the boy's school blazer to something familiar to the poet from his own childhood. Connotations of manure also suggest the contempt he feels for this schoolboy.
    'Brown as barrowloads from the blue-bottled byre': another simile drawing on his childhood surroundings. Alliteration links the words together, showing that in his memory the manure, blue-bottles and the byre are all connected together.

- *How many punctuation and sentence structure techniques can you find in Douglas Dunn's poem?*

    Line 5: parenthesis: dash introduces a fuller description of the school uniform and in turn brings to mind the childhood incident with the 'city cousin'. The second dash at the end of line 8 returns to the scene on the bus.
    Semi-colons in line 10 and line 13: semi-colon often suggests a close link between two points, such as cause and effect.

English Language Skills for Intermediate Level — Answers and Marking Schemes © Hodder Gibson.

Listing structure in lines 20–25: way one clause merges into the next in a long sentence suggests how he keeps running, determined to win the race.

Line 25: anti-climax. Identity of the runner is entirely unexpected; the reader might have expected that the poet was going to satisfy his long-held grudge and would be vindicated.

CHILD WITH PILLAR BOX AND BIN BAGS

Questions (page 97)

1. *Describe the incident that this poem deals with.* (2 marks)

The poem describes a woman taking a photo of her child who is in a buggy (1 mark). The buggy rolls towards the kerb and the mother quickly catches it (1 mark).

Total: 2 marks

2. (a) *What was it that the poet found surprising?* (2 marks)

She found it surprising that the mother decided to take the photo in the shade, when the sun was shining brightly on the other side of the road.

Total: 2 marks

(b) *How is this reinforced by the sentence structure used in the opening line?* (2 marks)

The poem opens with 'but', an unusual opening word as this is normally a conjunction which links back to a previous point (1 mark). This gives the poem a sudden opening and emphasises the surprise that the poet feels (1 mark).

Total: 2 marks

3. (a) *Pick out four different details of the surroundings which she mentions.* (4 marks)

Victor Gold, the bookmaker's shop; the licensed grocers; Universal Stores closed for modernisation; the hoarding blocking the building work from view; tenement buildings; the pillar box at the corner; the pile of bin bags, etc
(*1 mark for each feature*)

Total: 4 marks

(b) *Choose two of these and comment on what they add to the atmosphere of the poem.* (2 marks)

Possibilities include:
The names 'Victor' and 'Gold' connect with the words 'conquering' and 'sunlight'. They suggest success and prosperity, qualities which seem to be lacking in the rest of the scene, and which are alien to the mother.
The closed down shop, tenements, hoarding, bin bags, etc. suggest a run-down, poor area of the city where people feel they have few opportunities.
The pillar box might relate to the woman's decision to take the photograph: perhaps she intends to send it to someone. The reader might speculate further: is she sending the photo to the child's father, for instance?

Total: 2 marks

English Language Skills for Intermediate Level — Answers and Marking Schemes © Hodder Gibson.

4. *Much of the description in the poem is concerned with the contrast of light and shade. Quote an example of this contrast and comment on any aspect of the word choice used.*

(4 marks)

Note that an example of contrast will include **two** references: one to light and one to shade.

For example, on the 'shadowed street-side' there are the tenements, the shop closed for modernisation, the blank hoarding and the bin bags; on the sunny side there is the book-maker's and licensed grocers (2 marks). It is implied that these businesses are prosperous at the expense of the buildings opposite. Perhaps the profits being made from gambling and alcohol are at the expense of the poverty on the other side (2 marks)? Alternatively, the fact that the mother chooses to take the picture 'in the shadowed corner' may reflect the 'shadows' or suffering in her own life (2 marks).

Total: 4 marks

TIP

In textual analysis there are rarely 'right' or 'wrong' answers. Acceptable answers are opinions which are backed up convincingly with evidence from the text.

---

5. *The technique of alliteration is used several times in this poem.*

(a) *Quote an example of this.* (1 mark)

'shadowed street-side' (line 1); 'the baby in his buggy' (line 14).

Total: 1 mark

(b) *Comment on the effect the poet is aiming at.* (2 marks)

The use of alliteration often creates some kind of link or connection between the words: the baby and the buggy, for example, are almost like one thing. Similarly, the alliteration of 'shadowed street-side' links these three words together and suggests that the gloom pervades the whole street.

Total: 2 marks

6. (a) *What happens in lines 14–18?* (2 marks)

As the mother is about to take her photo the buggy begins to roll towards the kerb; she is very quick to grab hold of it, pull the brake on and prepare to take the picture again.

Total: 2 marks

(b) *Comment on any aspect of the poet's use of language to convey a sense of danger in these lines.* (3 marks)

The use of the simile 'it was fearful as Niagara' conveys a sense of danger (1 mark). The busy traffic pouring down the road is compared to the water cascading down Niagara Falls (1 mark). The implication is that in both cases crossing would be a highly dangerous escapade. The mother's awareness of the danger is stressed by the speed with which she reacted: 'she crossed the ground in no time' (1 mark).

Total: 3 marks

English Language Skills for Intermediate Level — Answers and Marking Schemes © Hodder Gibson.

7. *What point do you think the poet is making in the final four lines?* (3 marks)

The sun shines equally on everyone and everything: people, dogs, bin bags; nevertheless, it was the woman's choice to be on the shaded side of the street – she could just as easily have taken her photo on the other side.
The last line suggests that there may be no significance to this at all: the mother might not have made a conscious decision to photograph her child there, but simply took the picture at random.
(*1 to 3 marks depending on how well the point is developed*)

Total: 3 marks

8. *Talking about this poem, the poet, Kathleen Jamie, said: 'That listing, piling way of writing, with many concealed and half-rhymes, I find suspiciously quick and easy.' Find examples of this feature of her writing from anywhere in the poem and comment on whether you think it is effective.* (3 marks)

Listing structure is used in lines 21, 25, 27, etc.
Sometimes this gives an impression of several things going on at one time (line 21).
It can also convey a panoramic view, as if the poet's eye is ranging over all the features of the scene (as in lines 25–7).

Total: 3 marks
TOTAL MARKS: 30

UNLUCKY BOAT

Questions (page 98)

1. *Comment on the effectiveness of the first sentence as an opening to the poem.* (2 marks)

Many possible answers: two points for 1 mark each:
    abrupt / direct / simple language
    short / factual / summarises the rest of the poem
    creates a mood of sadness / gloom
    reference to the use of personification
    illustrates the truth of the title
    reference to the tone of 'that boat'

More obvious or less convincing points might gain a half mark each: e.g.
    short sentence
    clearly states what happened
    creates suspense

Total: 2 marks

2. *Without using quotations, summarise how each of the three men died.* (6 marks)

Sib hammered a nail through his thumb while constructing the boat (1 mark). He later died of blood poisoning at home, the treatment having failed to save his life (1 mark).
Mansie was casting spells on fish (1 mark) when the boat suddenly lurched and threw him into the water where he drowned (1 mark).
Angus was coming home drunk from the market (1 mark) when he fell over the remains of the boat which was lying among the rocks and broke his neck (1 mark).

Total: 6 marks

English Language Skills for Intermediate Level — Answers and Marking Schemes © Hodder Gibson.

3. *What is there in the poem to suggest the people are superstitious?* (2 marks)

'tinkers making the sign of the cross' (1 mark).
Reference to trying to catch a fish by putting spells on them (1 mark).
(This line can also be taken metaphorically.)

Total: 2 marks

4. *Boats are commonly referred to as 'she' rather than 'it'. How does the poet develop this use of personification throughout the entire poem?* (4 marks)

'She dipped a bow'; 'hauled her up'; 'there she lies'; 'leprous, unlucky bitch'
(*up to 2 marks for references alone*)
Other 2 marks for appropriate comments (e.g. connotations of 'leprous' – diseased, something to be shunned, etc; 'she dipped a bow' – suggestion of a deliberate action, etc.)

Total: 4 marks

5. *How is the sudden nature of Mansie's death conveyed?* (2 marks)

Reference to 'his pipe still in his teeth' (1 mark) plus fuller explanation of this (1 mark).

Total: 2 marks

6. *Why do you think the angels are described as 'cold' and 'green'?* (2 marks)

Connection of these adjectives with the sea (1 or 2 marks depending on how well explained): connotations of 'cold' – heartless, unfeeling, etc (1 mark). More able pupils may be able to recognise the technique of transferred epithet here.

Total: 2 marks

7. *To what extent does the poem convince you that the deaths of the men were caused entirely by the boat?* (4 marks)

A combination of reference / quotation and comment is required here.
Evidence for deaths being caused by the boat: significance of the opening line, 'she dipped a bow', and so on.
Evidence on the other side: detailed development of the point that each man had done something which helped to bring about his death.

Total: 4 marks

TIP

When a question contains the words 'to what extent' the answer should look at *both sides*; in this case, how far the deaths were caused by the boat and how far they were not.

---

8. *The language of the poem is a mixture of poetic description and imagery on the one hand and simple, colloquial language on the other. Find an example of each type of language and comment on the effectiveness of each.* (4 marks)

One example of descriptive language (1 mark) plus comment (1 mark) and an example of colloquial language (1 mark) plus comment (1 mark).

Total: 4 marks

English Language Skills for Intermediate Level — Answers and Marking Schemes © Hodder Gibson.

9. One critic has written that 'George Mackay Brown looks at people involved with the elements. In the settled Orkney communities, men and women ... gain hard-earned livelihood between fertile fields and the sea where tragedy is never far away. The poet shares many of the experiences of the people about whom he writes.'

    How far do you feel that these comments apply to 'Unlucky Boat'?   (4 marks)

    (This kind of question often produces vague answers. The following is an example of a good answer by a very able pupil. Note that for the full four marks examples and quotations should be included.)

    These comments do apply to the poem. The deaths of the three men all give information about different occupations in the community: Sib is a boatbuilder and crofter, Mansie a fisherman and Angus is probably a small farmer or crofter coming back from market. The work of all of them involves close interaction with the natural world. In the case of Mansie's death, he is 'ushered' to 'meet the cold, green angels', in a way a fitting end for a fisherman who has an innate bond with the sea. The sea is merely claiming its own. The drowning also emphasises the frequency of tragedy in Orkney. Moreover, the use of first names helps the reader to feel that these were real people and that the poet knew them personally and shared their experiences. The superstitious tone of the poem shows that Mackay Brown is sensitive to the thoughts and feelings of Orkney people and perhaps agrees with their feelings about the boat.

    (Such answers are rare and the marker would probably regret that no more than four marks could be awarded!)

                                                                          Total: 4 marks
                                                                          TOTAL MARKS: 30

THE LOVE SONG OF J. ALFRED PRUFROCK

Questions (page 101)

1. *What is the comparison suggested in lines 2–3?*   (2 marks)

    The evening is compared to a patient who has been put under anaesthetic and is lying on an operating table.

                                                                          Total: 2 marks

2. *What are the implications of this for the mood of the rest of the poem?*   (2 marks)

    The patient would be apprehensive about what was going to happen; the comparison implies that the character in the poem is about to undergo some painful experience.

                                                                          Total: 2 marks

3. (a) *What kind of area do the characters walk through?*   (2 marks)

        The area seems to be a rundown part of the town which is not frequented much at this time of evening.

                                                                          Total: 2 marks

English Language Skills for Intermediate Level — Answers and Marking Schemes © Hodder Gibson.

(b) *Select two descriptive details from lines 4–7 and comment on how they add to your impression of the area.*   (2 marks)

'One-night cheap hotels': these could be accommodation for people like travelling salesmen who only stay in the town briefly before moving on; they could also be the kind of places where men go with prostitutes.

OR

'sawdust restaurants': cheap restaurants with sawdust on the floor; 'oyster shells' suggests the location could be in a port and these cafés could be the kind frequented by sailors.

OR

'the streets that follow . . . intent' (lines 8–9): gives the impression that the streets are long and winding and that one could possibly get lost.

Total: 2 marks

4. *What might the 'overwhelming question' be (line 10)?*   (2 marks)

A proposal of marriage is a possible explanation.

Total: 2 marks

5. *Consider the effect of any aspect of sentence structure, sentence length and punctuation in lines 1–12.*   (3 marks)

Possibilities include:
Repetition: 'Let us go . . .' conveys a sense of determination or purpose; alternatively, it could represent reluctance on the part of the other unidentified character: she has to be persuaded to set off.
Semi-colons: these divide the verse into sections, suggesting a sequence building up to the climax of the 'overwhelming question'.
Ellipsis: the three dots leave the reader to speculate on what the question might be.
Anti-climax: 'O do not ask what is it': we are not told what the question is.
(*3 marks could be gained in various ways: one for each brief point; two for a more fully developed one, etc.*)

Total: 3 marks

6. *How has the setting changed in lines 13–14?*   (2 marks)

Lines 1–12: outdoors; lines 13–14: indoors.
Lines 1–12: quiet; few people ('half-deserted streets'); lines 13–14: busy; sense of movement ('come and go')

Total: 2 marks

7. *Why might the women be talking of Michelangelo?*   (2 marks)

This might suggest that the gathering is some kind of cultural party; it could be taking place in an art gallery.

Total: 2 marks

English Language Skills for Intermediate Level — Answers and Marking Schemes © Hodder Gibson.

8. (a) *Comment in detail on the comparison used in lines 1–22.* (3 marks)

Answers might refer to the use of personification or extended metaphor (1 mark for identifying technique): fog is characterised as a creature rubbing against the windows and infiltrating the atmosphere of the gathering (2 marks for detailed comment).

Total: 3 marks

(b) *What kind of atmosphere is created in these lines? Comment In detail on the poet's word choice.* (3 marks)

Words like 'lingered' and 'fell asleep' give the impression of a slow, lazy, sleepy atmosphere.

At the same time, words like 'rubs', 'licked' and 'slipped' suggest that the creature, or the fog, is moving about.

'Yellow fog', 'drains' and 'soot' have overtones of something dirty and unpleasant.

(*Up to 3 marks depending on quality of the commentary on the connotations of individual words or phrases*)

Total: 3 marks

9. *What connections might there be between the three sections of the poem?* (3 marks)

First section takes place outside: the characters' journey.

Second section: the atmosphere inside the venue they arrive at.

Third section: the view out of the window from inside the place where the social gathering is being held. The fact that the narrator has time to comment on the fog in such detail suggests that he feels isolated and is not fully involved in what is going on.

(*1 mark for each section, or 2 for more detailed comment on one section*)

Total: 3 marks

10. *Who do you imagine is the narrator in this poem? Is there any point at which the narrative point of view changes?* (2 marks)

Narrator may be the man who is going to the social event and who is hoping to ask his 'overwhelming question'. In lines 1–12 first person is used ('you and I'); last section is in third person.

Total: 2 marks
TOTAL MARKS: 28

English Language Skills for Intermediate Level — Answers and Marking Schemes © Hodder Gibson.